GW00889935

Circular Wal
Bakewell

Circular Walks around Bakewell

100 miles in the Peak District

by
George Hyde

Dalesman Books
1984

The Dalesman Publishing Company Ltd.,
Clapham, via Lancaster, LA2 8EB

First published 1984
© George Hyde, 1984

ISBN: 0 85206 786 0

Cover photograph of Beresford Dale near Hartington by the author.

Printed by Alf Smith & Co., Bradford

Contents

For those more interested in walking than sight-seeing the walk could be done in say, eight days — by telescoping the first three days, and days 6-8 into two days respectively, producing the following mileages:-

Bakewell to Longnor	14 miles
Longnor to Mapleton or Ashbourne	16-17 miles
Bakewell to Castleton	14 miles
Castleton to Hathersage	14½ miles

This arrangement would also allow for shorter walks on the fourth and eighth days to permit time for travel home. It will therefore be apparent that circular walks can be undertaken for four, five, eight or ten days according to the time available or one's inclination. Similarly, two or three days excursions can be done from the written route by the judicious use of public transport.

Acknowledgements — My thanks to Richard and Mary for their valued assistance in the surveying of the two routes.

Key to Sketch Maps

Path to be followed .... – – – – – –

Roads .... ——————

Alternative paths ....

Route of Trails .... – · – · – ·

Church .... +

Public House .... PH

Building .... ▬

River/Stream .... ⌇⌇⌇

Railway station .... —⊖—

(North approximates edge of page)

The route follows definitive rights of way as they existed at the time of the survey in 1982/83. Ramblers should be aware that the law allows public paths to be diverted or extinguished after due legal process, so it is possible that minor changes of route may be necessary in the course of time.

Introduction

THIS 100 mile route (or two 50 mile circular walks) in the Peak District of Derbyshire is intended for those country-lovers who may have heard of this fine walking territory — but never sampled it and those who have seen a little of the Derbyshire countryside and wish to see more.

My primary purpose in writing up this particular route has been to introduce what I consider to be some (but no means all) of its varied countryside — dales, hills, moorlands, trails, gritstone edges as well as country houses and some of the area's most attractive villages and market towns.

My acquaintance with the Peak District goes back to the late '40s and early '50s and, although since that time I have lived and walked in other parts of the country, I find myself still coming back every so often to its varied scene where I first learned to read map and compass.

Geologically the Peak District National Park area is divided between the Dark Peak — the rugged high gritstone country lying roughly to the north of a line between Chapel-en-le-Frith and Castleton, and south of this line the White Peak — so named after the white-grey limestone outcrops midst the softer contours of green countryside.

The Peak District National Park covers 542 square miles, mostly in Derbyshire, with outer fringes in Cheshire, Staffordshire and South and West Yorkshire. It was the first National Park to be designated by the National Parks Commission in 1949 and is now one of ten such areas so designated where special care is taken to conserve and enhance the natural beauty of the countryside and make provision for its enjoyment. Though classified as a 'National' Park, this does not signify that the land is nationalised — most is privately owned.

The National Park is administered by the Peak Park Planning Board, two-thirds of its members being appointed by constituent local authorities and the remaining one-third by the Secretary of State for the Environment. The Peak Park Office is at Aldern House, Baslow Road, Bakewell, Tel: 4321.

Information: There are three Peak Park information centres, all of which are on the chosen route:

1. Bakewell — Old Market Hall (tel. 3227) (Closed Wed. — Thurs.)
    Open — April-October incl. 10 a.m. to 6.0 p.m.
    Nov.-March incl. 10 a.m. to 5.0 p.m.

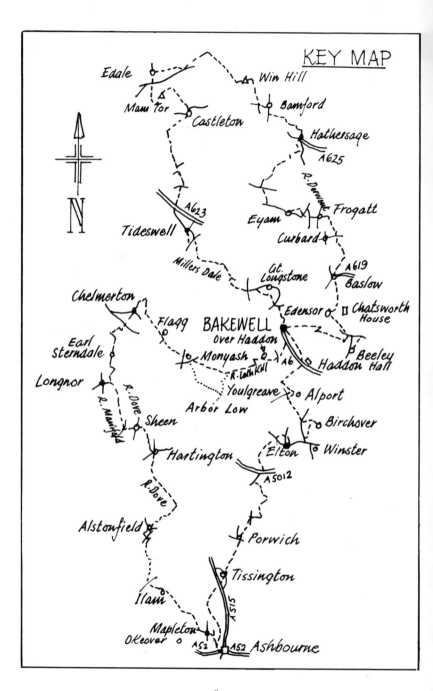

KEY MAP

2. Castleton — Castle Street (tel. Hope Valley 20679)
      Open — April-October incl. 10 a.m. to 6.0 p.m.
               Winter weekdays — 10 a.m. to 5.0 p.m.
3. Edale — Fieldgate (tel. Hope valley 70207)
      Open daily 9.0 a.m. to 5.30 p.m.
   All centres close for lunch between 1.0 and 2.0 p.m.

There is also a Tourist Information centre in Ashbourne at 13 Market Street (tel. 43666).

Accommodation: There is generous provision throughout the Park area of all kinds of accommodation — bed and breakfast, public houses, hotels, youth hostels, camping and self-service. For a few pence — a leaflet, 'Accommodation and Catering', can be obtained from any of the above centres.

The Ramblers' Association also publish a Bed and Breakfast Guide of Accommodation throughout Britain, which may be obtained from 1/5 Wandsworth Road, London SW8 2LJ (01-582-6878). If your visit is during the summer months it is advisable to obtain this information in advance and fix up beforehand.

Armed with these publications it is probable that, out of season, small parties of say two or three persons could get accommodation by telephoning one or two days ahead of intended arrival.

Transport: Though not on the railway network, Bakewell is served by express bus services from Nottingham and Derby to Manchester, and a fairly frequent service from Sheffield. Buxton is served by train from Manchester (Piccadilly) — with bus service down to Bakewell.

If your home town connects more conveniently with say, Ashbourne, there is a limited-stop service from Derby to Buxton — the walk could be started at Day 4 and end on Day 3. Similarly, train travellers from either Manchester or Sheffield could alight at Edale or Hathersage and do the walk from Day 8 or 9 and finish at Day 7 or 8. Having said that, however, I do strongly recommend Bakewell as the obvious central base from which to start the walk.

Bus time-tables for travelling to and within the Peak Park are available from the Planning Board H/Q, and the information centres referred to above.

Maps: The walk is covered by Map Nos. 110 and 119 of the O.S. 1/50,000, 2nd series, or the O.S. one-inch Tourist Map of The Peak District, with the exception of a small area one mile north from Ashbourne.

The sketch drawings of each day's walk are not to scale and are intended only as a general indication of the route.

Navigation: A compass is always a useful aid when walking in the countryside and is essential in low cloud and misty conditions.

Clothing: As most if this walk is in limestone country, walking conditions are generally favourable. Apart from long dry periods there are inevitably a few damp pockets here and there which call for light boots or strong shoes. For unsettled weather conditions, a cagoule and water-proof over-trousers are desirable.

Abbreviations: in the text: GR — Grid reference; N — north; E — east; S — south; W — west; FP — footpath; BW — bridleway; PH — public house; NT — National Trust; YH — Youth Hostel.

Bakewell: By virtue of its position and facilities, Bakewell is the capital of the Peak District and the obvious choice for the headquarters of the Peak Park Planning Board whose office at Aldern House, Baslow Road is about ¼ mile north of the river bridge in the centre of the town. This most attractive market town sits astride the river Wye with a fine 15th century five-arched stone bridge, whilst ¼ mile to the north is a mid-17th century packhorse bridge. The church with its octagonal tower and spire sits on the hillside just west of the town centre and dates from the Norman period, being much altered in the 13th and 14th centuries. In the churchyard is the shaft of a Saxon cross, about eight feet in height and probably dating from the 8th century. The font is 14th century and in the Vernon chapel are tombs of the Vernon Family of Haddon Hall. At the main road junction in the centre is the *Rutland Arms Hotel* built in 1804. It was here in the 1850s that Bakewell tarts were first made (locally known as 'puddings'). The town is well known for its agricultural show held on the first Thursday in August. The Old Market Hall in Bridge Street is an attractive 17th century building which houses the Peak Park Information Centre. A visit here is strongly recommended before starting your walk — one can obtain a pictorial history of the Peak Park area, numerous maps and guides as well as accommodation leaflets and time-tables.

Walk One

Bakewell – Chelmorton – Hartington – Mapleton – Elton – Bakewell

Day One

Bakewell, Over Haddon, Lathkill Dale, Monyash, Flagg, Chelmorton

10 miles. (Map – O.S. 1:50,000 No. 119)

(Diversion up to Arbor Low is an additional 3¼ miles)

Start (GR 217685) by the Rutland Arms Hotel in the town centre.

WITH one's back to the hotel, go E towards the post office and turn right into Water Lane and ahead S to cross Granby Road — keep right by riverside and ahead between playing fields. The path continues between rear gardens, crosses Wye Bank and on between more gardens, passing through allotments to bend right and left on a concrete road and ahead for 50 yards or so to join the main road (A6).

Ahead for 40 yards to cross over road and go up 'Bridleway to Over Haddon' on a rough cart track that becomes a green lane higher up the slope. After ½ mile or so go through iron hand-gate into field and by fieldside (SW) for 250 yards to a road.

Turn left for 150 yards — then right up the by-road towards Over Haddon. After about 400 yards (where the road bends right) go over wall ahead on footpath which goes diagonally to a stile, and ahead to cross over wall to the right of a fieldgate. Ahead W to pass an old elm tree and into the village by the Lathkill Dale PH.

Over Haddon is a high upland limestone village set in the midst of stone-walled fields on a terrace high above the river Lathkill. Keep ahead W up to the main street and along to the end where the road bends left to go steeply down to the riverside. (An appreciable length of the dale is now a National Nature Reserve.) The riverside path goes forward right from the Lathkill Lodge and ahead for 1¼ miles to leave the woods and enter an open steep sided valley. A further ⅔ mile ahead brings you to a footbridge on the left at the entrance to Cales Dale.

Here we have a choice — either to continue up the Dale (NW and W) for 1¼ miles to enter Monyash village — or to make a diversion of 3¼ miles to the SW to visit Derbyshire's 'Stonehenge', **Arbor Low,** which is the county's most important archaelogical monument, dating back to the Neolithic period (1600-2000 BC). The route is as follows:

After crossing the footbridge the path climbs steeply up the right-hand side of Cales Dale and bears right towards One Ash

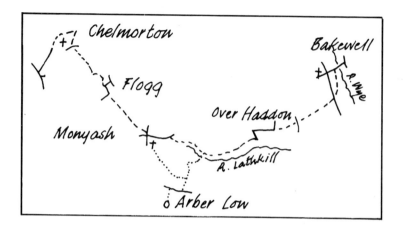

Grange Farm. Go up steps by a barn and ahead to a 'T' junction of farm roads where you turn sharp left — to pass cottages on your left — then right to pass round the side of a forge building on the right. Go through fieldgate (S) and uphill to join a farm road going in a similar direction and ahead along same for 600 yards to pass Cales Farm on left and barns to right. Ahead to road and turn right for ½ mile where turn left along entrance road to Oldhams Farm. On approaching farm, follow way-marking from the small car park to the stone circle. On a clear day there are extensive all-round views, and it will be seen from the map that a Roman road passes the site a ¼ mile to the SW, with Gib Hill tumulus site in between.

To get to Monyash from here, return to the access road to Cales Farm at GR 167640. Follow it for 300 yards to the second wall on your left where bear left alongside same (NW) for 350 yards. In the third field keep ahead, going down, then up to the far corner, then ahead in NW direction across several fields and down into a dry hollow — Fern Dale. Keep ahead to join a green lane (waymarked 28) which goes mostly NW for nearly ½ mile to a post on left (probably a finger-post) and cross over wall to right. Make for corner of stone walls (NNW) — then by fieldside and over several stiles to enter churchyard and into the village street in **Monyash.** The village lies at the W entrance to Lathkill Dale. It was at one time a market town and an important lead-mining centre. There is a shop and a 17th century PH — *The Bulls Head* — whilst nearby on the village green is the shaft of an old cross. A well-dressing ceremony is held at the end of May and beginning of June. (Bus service to Buxton via Flagg and Chelmorton.)

From the Green (Just beyond the PH) turn right along Chapel Street for 150 yards to FP (set back on left) and make for houses ahead — passing round same — then diagonally left (WNW) across several small fields to reach a rough metalled road. Bear right on same for ¼ mile to a junction with a barn on left, where you take the left fork (NW) for ¼ mile to enter a field. Bear slightly right (with Knotlow Farm further to the right) making for an ash clump ahead by the farm road. Keep ahead (NW) along road for 350 yards to join a road on a bend and ahead to where the highway bends to the right.

From this point the village of **Flagg** lies a little distance to the NE. It is a long-straggling and rather austere village set in the limestone uplands. There is a PH at the S end of the village. From the road bend we continue — almost N — on FP through stile and on through a gap into the next field where the path goes towards the wall on right by the village street. However, keep in this field and go NW to pass through more stiles — making for a copse ahead. Pass round the left side of the trees, cross over a wall and make for the right side of tree belt ahead. Keep ahead (NW) over several fields making for farm buildings on skyline (High Stool Farm).

On reaching road by farm, cross over, enter field to right of farm entrance road, and immediately left over wall. Keep to right of mounds to reach gateway into a large field. Go forward right (NW) to a stile — then diagonally across the next field to wall crossing in far corner. In the next field bear slightly right, making for a tree ahead by wall crossing. When in the large field ahead keep in the same direction but gradually veer away from the wall on your right to eventually reach the diagonal corner where you join a road. Turn left for 150 yards, then right up the Taddington road. After 400 yards keep ahead at fork to continue N for ¼ mile, and turn left on BW to go over bumpy ground for 400 yards when you suddenly drop steeply into Chelmorton (known locally as Chelly).

Chelmorton is Derbyshire's highest village, lying below two ancient tumuli on the summit of Chelmorton Low. The church stands some 1200ft. above sea-level being probably England's highest parish church — and dates from the 12th and 15th centuries. The walls are lined with ancient coffin-lids. The *Church Inn* is a most pleasant hostelry. The main village street follows a stream called the Illy Willy Water which we follow down to the road junction at the bottom. (GR 110695).

(There is a bus service to Buxton).

Day Two

Chelmorton, Earl Sterndale, Longnor, Manifold Valley, Sheen and Hartington.

9½ miles (Map – O.S. 1:50,000 119).

Start GR 110695.

FROM the bottom of the village street, cross over the Flagg road to a FP over the wall to right of field-gate and go up to the diagonal corner. Continue SW across the next field to enter a steeply sloping pasture to descend into a dry valley. Go up by wall on right for 60 yards to bear right through gap to a field-gate ahead and then on to a stepped stile between two field-gates to enter a large flat topped field. Continue SW to far corner, cross over a green lane and stile ahead and down by wall to the main road (A515).

Cross over road to the 'FP to Longnor' which goes through a small plantation to enter a field. Keep alongside wall to the right and at the end turn right along by mineral railway for ¼ mile. Diversions and closures of rights-of-way have been made since I first walked in this area some 35 years ago to accommodate this ever-expanding I.C.I. industrial complex. Although the site area has been excluded from the official boundary of the Peak Park, it is physically and scenically a part of the National Park and it is therefore fit and proper that walkers out to enjoy the countryside should experience the impact of such an incongruous intrusion into what was once a rural setting. However, we have to get through it as best we can!

After ¼ mile by the line, turn left over bridge — then immediately right alongside wall to a small shelter. (These huts are for public use after the warning siren has sounded for blasting purposes). Turn left along by another wall (SW) for 350 yards to repeat the right-left dog-leg in the next field. At the top go right and almost immediately left by fence line to reach a green lane.

Turn left for nearly ½ mile to a concrete shelter on left (and a gate ahead) where turn right on FP to go SW by fence line. At the top of a steep slope, bear slightly left across the hillside — then right — down a shallow gulley making for the left side of a detached house by the road. Continue left along road into Earl Sterndale to reach the church and bear right into the main village street by the *Silent Woman* PH (without her head!) This is a friendly pub for walkers.

Earl Sterndale is a small, almost hidden village amidst several curiously shaped limestone hills — Chrome Hill, Parkhouse Hill, Hitter Hill, Aldery Cliff and High Wheeldon. The last named was given to the National Trust as a monument to the members of the Derbyshire and Staffordshire Regiment who fell in the second world war. The church is early 19th century and was bombed in the last war and restored in 1952.

Take the FP on the NW side of the PH up a field and through a stile and ahead SW — soon to bear left round a mound on the E flank of Hitter Hill. Keeping left, go through another stile to go downhill across the contours (S) to a stile by an ash tree, cross over a field to a house ahead in a lane. Turn left along lane for nearly ½ mile to where the track begins to bend left, but you turn right down a green lane (SW) for 300 yards to cross over the river Dove by a wooden bridge on the county boundary. Continue up sloping field and then down — making for the right side of a barn ahead. Pass round the barn to left to join a rough road which goes uphill to enter Longnor village. After a short distance turn right down an asphalt path to the main street, then right for 150 yards or so to the old market place.

Longnor is a long street of gritstone houses on a high terrace just below the high ridge between the Dove and Manifold rivers with

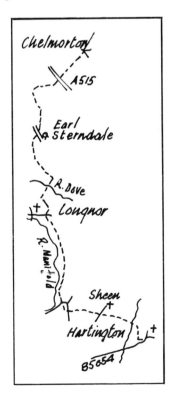

splendid views over the countryside to the SW. It was once a market town — the Market Hall (1873) overlooks the village centre. The church was rebuilt in the 18th century. There are several shops and inns in the village.

(The Buxton to Hartington bus service passes through the village.)

To continue the walk, retrace steps from the centre up the main road (E) to about 80 yards beyond the *Cheshire Cheese* PH where you cross the road into a lane (FP) to go SE down to a farm. Keep left through farm-yard — go over wall and make for the gap ahead by following wall on your left.

The path contours along the side of the valley on a fairly well defined route passing through many stiles in a generally SE direction for ⅓ mile to reach Crofts Farm where you dog-leg right-left. Follow the signs here and, when half-way along the next hedge, go through stile on left to continue along its other side. Keep to right side of derelict barn and ahead through several stiles to Over Boothlow Farm where you pass between the buildings. In the next field go forward right to about half-way along the hedge ahead and on to Lower Boothlow Farm. You then pass through more stiles after an iron field-gate before reaching Ridge End Farm on your left. Two fields ahead you cross a stream (by Pool Farm), go up bank, bear left at top and ahead S through more stiles to reach the riverside. A ¼ mile ahead (after meeting the river again), bear left up cart track and on to reach a road at a junction. Turn sharp right (towards river bridge) for about 25 yards — then left over stile, cross over stream and up slope (SE) to stile and ahead to field-gate on the road at Brund. Ahead up road for 100 yards to bear left up track (BW) between hedgerows on banks. Some 350 yards on — after passing the hill tumulus on your left — take the FP which runs parallel to the left side of the BW and ahead (E) through more stiles to reach the road in **Sheen** village. The main street runs N — S along a low ridge with fine views over Dovedale to the E and N. The church was rebuilt in the last century in Gothic design of the decorated period.

Turn left for 50 yards — then through the first gate on the right to pass by a house in field and downhill to the far corner to a stile. In the next field go ESE up then down to stile and continue through more stiles in the same direction to top of slope. Go down a hollow to a stile and over the next field to re-cross the county boundary via footbridge. Bear slightly right (SE) over three fields to reach a road serving industrial buildings. Turn left along road to reach the centre of Hartington (GR 128604). There are several shops, a Youth Hostel, a hotel and a PH in the village.

Hartington, originally a 13th century market town, is set amidst limestone hills and dales. It has many fine old stone houses — including the Old Hall (now the Youth Hostel) which dates from the early 17th century but was largely restored in the last century. On the

18

opposite slope is the early 14th century cruciform church with a fine perpendicular tower. The font is 15th century. The Victorian town hall is now used as a shop. The hotel is named after Charles Cotton, who with Izaak Walton used to fish the river Dove in Beresford Dale nearby. At the N end of the dale Cotton built a one-roomed fishing house in 1674. This is now hidden from view on private land. Well-dressing ceremony: September 11-19.

(Buses to Buxton via Sheen and Longnor, and to Ashbourne via Ilam and Tissington).

Day Three

Hartington, Beresford and Wolfscote Dales, Alstonfield, Hope, Ilam, Mapleton.

11 miles (Map O.S. 1:50,000 No.119)

(Diversion into Ashbourne and back – 2½ miles)

Start – GR 128604

FROM the *Charles Cotton Hotel* take the Warslow Road (B5054) SW for 50 yards or so to bear left (by toilets) on a path that goes to the right along a well-used route by a wall to your right. The path continues S for over ½ mile to enter woods at the head of Beresford Dale. In the first ½ mile or so the path crosses and recrosses the river Dove following which you enter Wolfscote Dale. After a further 1¼ miles you pass Biggin Dale on the left and, shortly after passing a path up to a cave (on the same side), you go right over stepping-stones to climb up across the contours of a grassy hill. The path starts in a S direction and slowly bends right as you climb up to go SW, then W to make for a wall crossing just to the right of the lowest point of the wall ahead. Keep ahead W and, after the next wall crossing, bear left (SW) and follow the waymarks to a barn, passing to the S side of same. Continue SW on farm track for ¼ mile to join a track coming from the right, bear left along same to reach a road where you turn right and into **Alstonfield** village. There is a PH and a shop in this pleasant upland limestone village which lies over the county boundary in Staffordshire. The church contains development of many periods back to Saxon times. There is a 17th century pew that was used by Charles Cotton over 300 years ago. The poet entertained his friend and brother angler Izaak Walton at Beresford Hall now demolished.

Continue W through the village to the school on the W side of the Hartington Road. Follow the FP alongside the school, cross over playing field and go diagonally right in the next field and down to cross over a lane. Keep ahead by wall to another stile and turn left alongside wall and ahead for 250 yards to a road. (The small hamlet of **Hope** lies over the road to the SE). Turn right and keep left at fork to pass *The Watts Russell* PH in Hopedale and ahead on road for 200 yards to a FP on the right. Proceed SW up a grassy hollow for 150 yards, then gradually bear right steeply up to a stile and on to a road.

Turn left for 15 yards, then cross over to FP on right to go up by wall and further stiles ahead (SW). In the third field, go forward left to meet wall and uphill by same through several fields to where the contours begin to level out — when you bear left to a gate into a green lane. Cross over same and ahead SW with wall on your right for 250

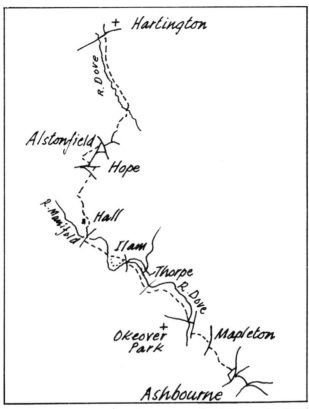

yards — then left by Old pits and cross next field diagonally (SE). Go by wall (S) to a field-gate and ahead but keep away from the wall on your left — down to another field-gate. In the next field, avoid left fork uphill, and keep by wall along a high terrace path with extensive views S and W over the Manifold valley. Soon the path bends left to reach Castern Hall — an imposing Georgian House. Continue down the twisting drive to just before a pair of stone gate posts, where you fork right on a FP down across two fields to Rushley Bridge.

Cross the river Manifold and up a by-road for 150 yards where you take FP on left (just before a farm). Ahead (SE) over a wet patch — up a bank through a stile and ahead over the next field to go through gateway. Make for another field gap and ahead down slope to a footbridge to recross the river Manifold.

Turn right here, where you have a choice of either going on the lower path to enjoy the river scene to reach Ilam Hall or going forward left up slope and over the hill, thus cutting the distance. Ilam Hall is a Youth Hostel, and also contains a NT shop, and a cafe which is open during the summer months. The Hall was built during the last century in the Tudor-Gothic style by Jessee Watts-Russell. The Hall and grounds were given to the National Trust by Sir Robert McDougall. Mr. Watts-Russell also re-built the village. The church, though much restored at the end of the last century, is of interest — having a Norman font and a 13th century tomb — whilst the churchyard has some interesting trees and two stone Saxon crosses.

To continue the walk go down path along the N side of the church and left on path into Ilam village. Follow the main street (E) but where the road bends left, keep ahead to cross over Ilam Bridge and go immediately left down to the river-side path. After a mile or so you reach Coldwall Bridge where you keep ahead on the west bank. After leaving a wooded area and entering meadow land keep near to the woods on right, and from here on the path is fairly clear ahead to Littlepark Farm (on left) where you join a farm road for about 100 yards before taking FP on left through hedgerow. Continue S across two fields to reach old stone buildings by roadside at Okeover. (A little distance to the west lies Okeover Hall (1780) set in pleasant parkland, whilst the nearby 14th century church houses memorials commemorating the Okeover family over many centuries). We turn left here to cross over the river Dove into Derbyshire again and fork right on FP which cuts the corner and leads to the *Okeover Arms* PH in Mapleton village. Lying on the E bank of the Dove in lush meadowland, **Mapleton** is a quiet village with a very small 18th century church surmounted by a curiously shaped octagonal dome. (GR165478).

Ashbourne lies 1¼ miles to the SE and for those wishing to visit or stay there, the route is as follows: From the PH continue S a short distance to a FP on left which climbs up the hill (E) then bears SE over the top and down to the Tissington Trail (the old railway line). Bear right on the Trail 100 yards or so, then left over footbridge. Keep ahead (S) in field, then bear left uphill (SE) making for the diagonal corner and ahead to reach a road in Ashbourne. Cross over to FP that goes down The Channel into the Market Place.

Ashbourne is a fine old market town which, lying at the southern end of the White Peak, acts as a gateway to the National Park. Dr. Johnson, James Boswell, George Eliot and Izaak Walton all had associations with the town. Boswell stayed at the old coaching inn, *The Green Man and Blacks Head*, a hostelry with much character, whilst Dr. Johnson used to visit his school friend, Dr. Taylor, at the 17th century house in Church Street. This particular street is probably the most varied and attractive in the whole county. The large cruciform church dates from the 13th century with later additions. The elegant spire is over 200ft. in height — being built in the 14th century. There are many fine alabaster and marble tombs dating from the 14th to 16th centuries, the most impressive being the white marble figure of a child, Penelope Boothby, sculptured by Thos Banks in 1791. Dr. Taylor, who died in 1788, is buried in the south transept.

Tourists information is provided in premises at 13 Market Street. (Bus routes: The Derby to Manchester service passes through the town. There is a limited service to Hartington with connection to Buxton).

Day Four

Mapleton, Tissington Trail, Tissington, Parwich, High Peak Trail, Gratton Dale, Elton.

13 miles (Map O.S. 1:50,000 119)

Start – GR 165478

A SHORT distance S of the PH turn left on FP which climbs up (E) and at the top bear right (SE) to go down to join the route of the old railway line — now known as the Tissington Trail. The line was constructed in 1899 and operated until 1963, running between Ashbourne and Buxton.

Turn left on the Trail and go N for some 3½ miles to the point where, looking forward left, you see the houses in Tissington village. Take FP on left (just short of a bridge crossing) over fence to go N over two fields. You then follow a high wall to your right, through a stile at the end and down into the village.

Tissington is a small estate village of the Fitzherbert family and is generally accepted as being Derbyshire's prettiest village. The manor house was built in 1611. Almost opposite is the church which was largely restored in the last century — but the tower, the main doorway and the font are of Norman origin. It has a two-decker oak pulpit of the 17th century. The village is famous for its well — dressing ceremony on ascension day — a ceremony dating back to the floral festivities of pagan days, to celebrate the continuing supply of clean spring water to the village.

From the small triangular green (near the church) go up the path to the church — but fork right before reaching the porch, go through wooden gate, then diagonally left to an iron fieldgate. Keep left up by wall to the top, cross a lane and ahead (N) to another lane and turn right on same for ⅓rd mile to cross over the Trail. The lane bends left and after 60 yards or so you take a FP on the right 'Footpath to Parwich'. This is a fairly well-used path to the NE going down, then up and finally down into the village — which has a PH and a shop.

Parwich is an attractive limestone village amidst lush pastures. The Victorian church (1873) is good for its period and contains some Norman work in the tower. The font was originally Norman. The 18th century Hall on the hillside is now used as a hospital. Leave the village by the road which goes along the N side of the church — but after 100 yards turn left up path, cross an estate road, go along a short drive and then via stepping-stones across a lawn and down a short drive to a road at a junction. Cross over to a short link road, into the

24

next road and turn left up same for about 200 yards, turn left on FP to ascend for 100 yards to a junction with a cul-de-sac where you turn sharp right up a metalled road to pass in front of some houses. Keep to the wall on your left where the FP bends left and enters a wood. Turn left steeply uphill and on reaching a more open area bear right on a terrace path — keeping wall on your left and turn northwards by the wall and across two stiles. The path then bends right (NE) — the wall crossings are unclear — but when you see a signpost ahead make for it to reach a road.

Turn left (N) along the road for 200 yards to a junction. Here turn right on a FP through a grassy hollow and ahead for ⅔ mile to a 'T' junction with a track. Turn left (N) along same through another valley for ½ mile to reach an outbuilding on left. A hundred yards

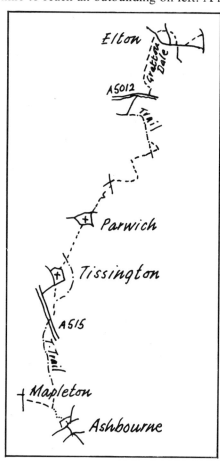

ahead, turn right over a wall and make for the diagonal corner of field. In the next field continue ENE by wall on left to the first field boundary where bear left to cross over a ladder-stile.

Continue E up slope to pass under stone built bridge which carried the former Cromford and High Peak railway and is now the High Peak Trail. You can — if you so wish — clamber up the embankment to the left, go through a small plantation and on to the High Peak Trail directly. An easier way, however, is to continue forward under the bridge and ahead for 250 yards where turn along a green lane to join the High Peak Trail on a bend near a disused quarry. The Cromford and High Peak railway ran for 17½ miles from Cromford to Dowlow near Buxton. The Trail connects with the Tissington Trail at Parsley Hay — some 5 miles to the NW. You follow the route of the former line for 1¼ miles N and W through scenic countryside with extensive views until you reach a picnic area and a car park by a road.

Turn right along metalled road for ¾ mile (NNE) to its junction with the main road (A5012). Unfortunately there is no right-of-way through Mouldridge Grange opposite, so you must walk along the main road E for ¼ mile where you turn left on a FP. Keep alongside wall (on left) and keep by same as it turns left — but after losing a little height bear right down a gulley into Gratton Dale. After 200 yards — at the point where the FP through Long Dale goes off to your left — keep ahead through hand-gate and continue down Gratton Dale to reach the road at Dale End, Gratton.

At telephone kiosk bear left along road for 60 yards, where turn right over fence and follow FP across marshy area and then forward right uphill to a stile. Continue ESE across several fields; pass a derelict stone building (on right) and keep ahead to a road. Turn right along road for 75 yards to cross the stile on left and go forward right uphill towards Elton church. On approaching buildings keep to left and along a short track to join a road and ahead up to the cross roads in the centre of Elton village.

Elton is an old lead mining village astride the 900ft. contour. The long ridge-top main street is also the divide between the gritstone and the limestone: villagers with gardens on the gritstone (north side) grow quite different flowers from those with limestone gardens on its south side. The church is 19th century, replacing one that collapsed — probably through lead-mining operations. (GR 222610).

(The YH is open at week-ends only).

Day Five

Elton, Birchover, Robin Hood's Stride, Youlgreave, Bradford Dale, Lathkil Dale, Haddon Hall, Bakewell

8 miles (Map – O.S. 1:50,000 119)

Start – GR 222610

FROM the church go E along the main street for ⅓ mile to a FP on left (just beyond a barn). Go forward right to pass through stiles either side of a house drive and ahead NE to a stile to left side of an ash tree and into a lane. Cross over onto a farm track (NE) which contours round a north slope and leads to opencast workings. Ahead there appears to have been some dispute as to the right-of-way — but no objection is made to crossing over post-wire fence on your right and continuing E over rough worked land to descend to a field-gate on to the B5056 road, by some buildings.

Turn right along road for 250 yards or so to a cross-road sign — where go left over low wall and down to a field-gate on to a by-road. Turn left along lane for 60 yards to first field-gate on left, enter field and walk a few yards NW to follow hedge round corner to right and ahead N to pass a stone ruin — then downhill to cross over a stone footbridge. Go uphill by another stone ruin and ahead to the left-hand corner of field (N) to cross a stone stile by a field-gate. Keep ahead up and across slope to the top with Rocking Stone Farm to your left.

Continue N down drive for 100 yards to where the drive bends to left, at which point you can decide whether to visit **Birchover** village — ¼ mile to the east. If so, walk down the stone flags in the grass to a drive and turn right along same for 300 yards to reach a PH at a road junction in Birchover. The village occupies a most favourable position on a high south-facing terrace with glorious views southwards. It is a good centre for visiting the numerous stone circles, monoliths and burial mounds to be found to the NE on Stanton Moor. The church lies in a hollow at the lower end of the main street and is mostly of the Victorian period. There are two inns and a shop in the village.

If not visiting the village, continue along the drive from Rocking Stone Farm — where the drive bends left and soon becomes a grassy track along a high terrace with good views (W) across to the gritstone rocks of Robin Hood's Stride and Gratcliffe Tor. The path skirts a plantation on the left before dropping down to the main road (B5056).

Go S along the road for 150 yards, then right into an access road and immediately right again up a private drive (FP) NW. After 300 yards — where you go between gate-posts — fork left on a grassy track track which leads up between the rock outcrops of Robin Hood's Stride (on left) and Gratcliffe Tor (to the right). The former is so named as that worthy gentleman is said to have jumped the 22 yards distance between the two highest rocks — whilst the latter is the site of a shallow cave where a hermit is said to have lived some 600 years ago.

At the top of the slope, keep ahead NW over two fields to cross over road and along the farm road to Harthill Moor Farm.

Follow the farm wall round to the left, cross over a wood stile and keep bearing slightly right to pass over two more stiles. In the next field you see Youlgreave village ahead and the general direction is NW towards the church tower. Cut across the slope downhill to a wood stile to left of iron field-gate, and in the next field go forward left on a double track which soon bends left.

In the next field, bear right to cross a wood fence and ahead to pass tree stumps and steeply down to cross a stream. Go diagonally over the next field to gate by wall and ahead to houses in Youlgreave where you bear right down to river crossing.

Turn left immediately after going over the water to walk alongside the river Bradford for about 200 yards — where fork right up asphalt path into a street and ahead to the main village street by the Old Hall.

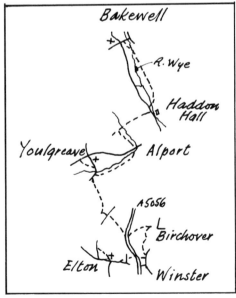

28

Youlgreave sits on a limestone ridge between the rivers Lathkill and Bradford. The church is one of the most interesting in The Peak — possessing a very fine 15th century square tower, some Norman work in the south arcade, and an unusually designed 12th century font which originally came from Elton church. There are also some very fine 15th century alabaster tombs. Restoration carried out in the last century was done most sensibly by Norman Shaw. Well-dressing ceremonies take place during the last week in June. There are several shops and PHs and a YH in the village, and a bus service to Bakewell.

Turn right along the village street for 200 yards or so to the crossroads with the church on right and *The George* PH on left. Go down by the side of the church (SE) — keep right at fork to reach the river crossing again. Go E through gateway (with stream on you right) soon to cross river and bend left by rock face. Keep to the path nearest the water for over ½ mile to reach the road in Alport — where the river Bradford joins the Lathkill. Cross over road (on a bend) to a FP which goes NW along the W bank of the Lathkill for about ½ mile to reach Raper Lodge (on left). Turn right (NE) down lane, cross river bridge and ascend through woodland to top. Keep left to halfway round spoil heaps to a stile on left and ahead by the same fence line to pass through a tree-belt (with farm buildings on right) to enter extensive pastures. Keep ahead NE over Haddon Pastures for 1 mile or so during which time Haddon Hall will come into view ahead, lying to the E side of the main road (A6).

Haddon Hall sits on a limestone slope above the river Wye. The Vernon and Manners families are responsible for most of this outstanding building which dates back to the 12th century. It was the 9th Duke of Rutland who restored the house to what it was in 1640. The long gallery upstairs is 110ft. in length — being extended in the 17th century, and it was during this period that the terraced gardens were laid out. The House is open April to September — daily (except Suns. and Mons.) 11 a.m.-6 p.m.

On joining the A6 road, turn left (N) for 250 yards to a FP on right through a stone stile and shortly cross over the river Wye. At lane crossing, dog-leg right-left and from here on the path is waymarked for the mile or so into the centre of Bakewell.

This brings us to the half-way stage — and those intending to tackle the second-half will find much of interest in Bakewell for an overnight stay. (A few notes on the town are to be found in the Introduction).

Walk Two

Bakewell – Tideswell – Edale – Hathersage – Baslow – Bakewell

Day Six

Bakewell, Great Longstone, Monsal Head, Millers Dale, Tideswell Dale, Tideswell

9 miles (Maps – O.S. 1:50,000 110 and 119)

Start – GR 217685

FROM *The Rutland Arms Hotel* in the town centre go N up the Buxton Road (A6) for ¼ mile to track on right (almost opposite old farm building on left) which goes over a 17th century packhorse bridge. Cross over a road and ahead up rough track through stone quarry and ahead through field-gate into a field. At the next field-gate go forward left (NW) on a grassy track over field. In the next field keep ahead with wall on right — making for right side of cottage ahead, where you pass through a kissing-gate in the wall. Make towards wood (NW) to meet same about 300 yards ahead by a stile on left to go through wall into rough wood-land. Go down through the wood to the bottom and across a field to reach a road by Rowdale House.

Turn left for 300 yards to junction and bear right to pass under railway bridge and immediately left on FP by foot of old railway embankment for 100 yards to cross over wall on right. We go almost N up this field towards Great Longstone. On reaching new housing estate at the junction of Croft Road and Edgeview Drive, bear right down to the village street and left up to the village centre. If not wishing to see the village, cross over Croft Road to FP that goes W to the playing field and ahead to Station Road.

Great Longstone is an attractive long-street village with many fine 18th century limestone houses. There are two inns and some shops. The church is 12th to 15th century — its most glorious feature being the 15th century roof with moulded beams with bosses of flowers. Opposite the 'Crispin Inn' is The Hall (1747) which has a red brick facade. (Buses to Bakewell are fairly frequent).

We leave the village via Station Road which goes S from the side of the *Crispin Inn*. After 200 yards go right on FP (which is opposite the path that cuts out the village street). This path goes just N of W across several fields for nearly ½ mile to reach the road in Little Longstone village. Keep ahead (W) on road for ½ mile to road junction by the *Monsal Head Hotel*. From the car park there is a most dramatic view of Millers Dale with the river Wye deep below.

From the N side of the hotel, take FP through wall on W side of car park to go immediately right steeply down to valley bottom —

turning left by farm building and cross over the river by footbridge. Go forward right on "Footpath to Breakfield' up across the slope to join the old railway track of the Midland line between Bakewell and Buxton and now in used as the Monsal Trail. The four tunnels on this route have had to be sealed, so the Trail is in four separate lengths linked by new paths or by road. The four sections are: Bakewell-Longstone (4 miles) Monsal Dale (1 mile), Millers Dale (2 miles) and Chee Dale (1 mile). A short distance ahead we reach the site of Monsaldale station where we go left on to a rough road and bear right to pass under the railway to drop to and over the river and ahead to road junction at Upperdale. Turn left along road for ½ mile to go alongside Cressbrook Mill to where just short of road fork ahead — go left through gateway of the old mill premises. The path bears right, goes over footbridge and under limestone cliffs by the riverside and ahead for 1¼ miles to reach Litton Mill where we join a road.

Keep ahead (W) for 350 yards to fork right on 'FP to Tideswell Dale'. The path soon bends right to go N up the dale for ¾ mile to reach a picnic area. Keep ahead N by a line of beech trees to join a road and uphill for 250 yards to FP on left (immediately past disposal works.) The path climbs a little before bending right to traverse the hill-side parallel to the road below and bends left when by the road junction. The path contours round to a field-gate and on to a farm track — then ahead to the village street and continue N to the centre of Tideswell. (GR 153757)

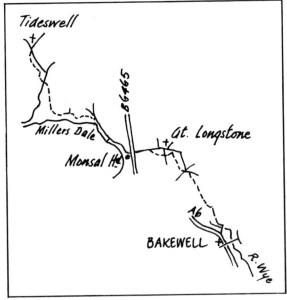

Tideswell, a large limestone village above the 900ft. contour, was once a market town. The magnificent 14th century parish church, St. John the Baptist, is known as the cathedral of the Peak. There is much to admire, the chief items being the tall perpendicular tower, the splendid chancel, the stone screen behind the altar and ten stalls in the transept with misericords — as well as various pre-reformation monuments and brasses. Next door is *The George* — an old coaching Inn (1730) — a building of character with some Venetian type windows. There are ample shops, several inns and eating establishments. The YH is at Ravenstor in Millers Dale. A wakes week is held at the end of June — when a well-dressing ceremony also takes place.

(The village is served by the Bakewell-Castleton bus service).

Day Seven

Old Moor, Castleton, Mam Tor and Edale

9 miles (Maps – O.S. 1:50,000 110 & 119)

Start – GR 153757

FROM the side of the church go up Pursglovee oad to join another main street and ahead N through Market Square to slowly climb uphill for over a mile to 'T' junction with the Chesterfield-Stockport Road (A623). Cross over up by-road for ⅔ mile to another 'T' juncion at Bushy Heath Farm. Turn right for 250 yards — then left up a rough road (NW) for ¾ mile to join a public road for 150 yards. Just beyond right bend, turn lef to continue NW for ⅔ mile over rough grassland to reach a fence line which runs along the 1500ft. contour — this being the highest point on our crossing of Old Moor. The path gradually loses height to pass through another gate and ahead — up slightly — then down to reach a multiple junction of paths.

Cross over walled track to go forward right through two gates in quick succession and bear slightly right (NE) along a grassy path on flat terrain for 350 yards to drop down a short slope. At this point the bridleway bears right to enter Cave Dale which eventually passes the ruins of Peveril Castle before reaching Castleton. The more attractive route, however, is to keep ahead on FP (NE), soon to see the impressive view ahead of Lose Hill (1563ft.), and later as we begin to lose height the village of Castleton in its setting of the Hope valley below. The FP is not clearly defined hereabouts, but keep left to go down and across the steep grassy slope — aiming for the village below. When about half-way down, make for the corner where the wall below to your left meets the foot of a wooded slope ahead where we enter a lane. Ahead over a bridge and through village street to reach Castle Street by the YH. Turn left here for the church and main road ahead.

Castleton is dominated by Peveril Castle (1176) but renowned for its several caves. The Peak Cavern — near the village centre — has a wide entrance which rises to almost 60 feet in the cliff face and contains a 400 year old ropewalk. The cave is open for guided tours from April to mid-September. The Blue John Caverns lie about a mile to the W and were originally worked for lead mining. The purple-blue fluorspar has been used for ornaments and jewellery since the early 18th century. It is thought that the Romans used this as a mine.

The nearby Speedwell Cavern — at the entrance to the Winnats Pass — consists of a half mile long underground canal which is reached by an old lead mine shaft. The Treak Cliff Caves — a little to the N — were opened in 1935 and are famous for the highly coloured stalagmites and stalactities which also contain some Blue-John.

The church was mostly re-built in the last century, but has a Norman chancel arch and a 15th century perpendicular tower. The village is well served with shops, cafes and inns. (There is a bus service to Sheffield).

We leave the village by the *Nags Head* PH at the junction of Back Lane with the main road (A 625) (GR 151829) to go N down main road to a rrigt-hand bend, where keep ahead (N) down Hollowford Lane for nearly ½ mile to bear left (when just past pavilion on right) along a lane sign-posted to 'Hollins Cross'. After ⅓ mile — where the lane bends left — we keep ahead over a stile to climb up across the contours to the shoulder of the ridge — known as Hollins Cross — midway between Lose Hill to the right and Mam Tor to the left. There are excellent views ahead over the Kinder Scout plateau beyond Edale village.

Go left along ridge for ¾ mile to reach the summit of Mam Tor (1695ft.) — the best known of the Derbyshire hills. It is known locally as the 'shivering mountain' because its E face is being slowly eaten away as the soft layers of shales wear away more quickly than the

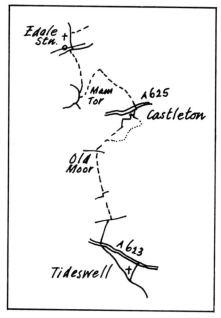

hard layers of gritstone which fall away for lack ot support. The summit was the site of an Iron Age fort.

From the top go SW down to a road, then right to a choice of paths to go N for a mile to join a road near Edale station. Turn right to junction, then left into the main village street in Edale. Near the station is the *Rambler Inn* — recently taken over by the Ramblers' Association — where refreshments and accommodation are provided. Further N on the opposite side of the road is the Information Centre and car park at Fieldsend.

Edale is a one-street village of gritstone houses up the valley of the Grindsbrook and fades out where the gradient becomes steep. The church is Victorian — whilst the *Old Nags Head* PH dates from the 16th century. (GR 123857)

The Youth Hostel lies 1¼ miles ENE of the village. The Pennine Way long distance footpath starts from the village on its 250 mile trek N into Scotland.

(Train service from Manchester and Sheffield).

Day Eight

Edale, Nether Booth, Roman Road, Win Hill, Thornhill, Bamford and Hathersage

10½ miles (Map – O.S. 1:50,000 110)

Start – GR 123857

WE leave the village by the FP (almost opposite the church) to go E to cross the Grindsbrook — keep left beyond the field-gate on main track to Ollerbrook Booth ¼ mile ahead. After a further 150 yards, avoid left fork up to farm and keep ahead across field to a gate. Bear slightly right in the next field and ahead E across three fields to reach a farm track which we follow for 100 yards or so. Where the track turns right we keep ahead E by fence line on left for ¼ mile to meet the road at *Nether Booth*. Continue E along road for 250 yards to fork left on 'Bridleway to Alport' up an overgrown gulley which climbs up to pass round the back of Clough Farm. On passing through field-gate keep ahead up along terrace path E for over ½ mile to the highest contour from where there are good views back to Mam Tor and the Edale valley, and S to the Hope valley. The path bends left at this point to go down across the contours to bottom of gully and turns acutely right — shortly to cross a stream by stepping-stones.

Go forward up slope (NE) for ⅓ mile to reach a low summit at a cross track and go over stile on right. For the next mile or so we follow the route of a Roman road (S) which presents a fine view of the Ladybower Reservoir to the SE. Some 250 yards ahead on passing through a gate we reach Hope Cross and continue with plantations to the left for almost ½ mile to go through another gate. The track now bears slightly left towards the side of the plantation and after ½ mile (where the woodland boundary turns slightly left) we go a little to the right along a grassy path. This keeps to the higher contour up the slope of Win Hill for ⅔rds mile to bend left (E) for ½ mile to climb the rocky outcrop to the summit (1516 ft). There are fine views in all directions and you will need a few minutes to identify all the landmarks.

We descend down the E side to a step-ladder over a wall where we bear left down through open woodland — soon to reach a post-wire fence. Turn right alongside same and at the end of the trees keep ahead on a grassy terrace path S with views down the Derwent valley ahead — whilst a back view over your left shoulder reveals the dam at the southern end of the reservoir.

When the path begins to lose height, walk along the bank on the left as the main path shortly bends right, and keep ahead S downhill

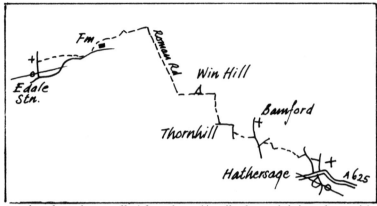

to a handgate by a wall. After about ¼ mile the path joins a lane with houses on left at Townbeck and ahead down to the main street in **Thornhill.** Bear left along the village street for 300 yards to a path on left (by Barleyland) to go SE down to join a metalled road by the side of Water Board premises. Bear left along the lane by playing fields, and cross over the river Derwent to meet the main road (A 6013)just S of Bamford. The village centre is about ¼ mile up the road to the left (N) where there are some shops and a PH.

Bamford is a hill-side village below Bamford Edge and overlooks the Derwent valley. The houses are gritstone and the church with its slim steeple is Victorian (1861) being built by Wm. Butterfield.

We turn right here along the main road for 300 yards to bear left up Saltergate Lane to a FP 350 yards ahead on right. The next ½ mile or so over the Golf course is rather tricky as the rights-of-way are not defined on the ground and therefore a compass is most helpful. The route goes forward left up slope for 300 yards (gradually moving away from the lane on our left) to a point about 80 yards short of a wooden shelter ahead, where we come to the route of a cross path that has come from near the road junction at the top of Saltergate lane over to the left. We turn right here to go SSE over the course making for another shelter ¼ mile ahead. After 200 yards or so the route drops down to cross over a stream by footbridge, bears left up slope and at the top keep left to go E and join a hedgerow on your left. Keep ahead to pass by the N side of old farm building and on to a stile and so leave the golf course.

In the field we go just S of east down to a stone stile and cross a stream by stones that go forward left and ahead uphill towards Thorpe Farm where we join a road to the left side of the buildings. Keep ahead uphill to 'T' junction at the top and bear right for 250 yards to go over stile on left. This path goes steeply down towards Hathersage ahead by crossing two fields almost diagonally — then slightly left to go over a road and ahead to a footbridge. Bear right, cross over a small paddock to join a rough farm track and turn right along same for ¼ mile to reach the main road (A 625) in Hathersage. (GR 232816)

Hathersage is a big village that has grown in recent years. The church which lies a little distance to the NE — being almost detached from the village — is attractive and dates from the 14th century and has a splendid 15th century tower. Little John is said to have been buried in the churchyard. The church has literary connections with Charlotte Bronte who wrote Jane Eyre when staying at the vicarage. There are many shops, several hotels and inns. (The YH is open weekends only).

The village gala usually takes place the first week in July. Hathersage is well served with public transport — being on the Sheffield/Castleton bus route, and the Sheffield/Manchester train service.

Day Nine

Hathersage, Bretton Clough, The Barrel Inn, Eyam, Froggatt, Curbar and Baslow Edge, Baslow

11½ miles (Maps – O.S. 1:50,000 110 and 119)

Start – GR 230815

FROM the front of the *George Inn* — at the junction of the A625 with the B6001 — cross over into the Bakewell Road and immediately fork right along Mill Lane. After passing the railway bridge, the lane bends left, shortly to reach the entrance to Nether Hall on right. Keep ahead over wall on a FP that goes SE for almost ½ mile through fields to rejoin the B6001 by Leadmill Bridge. Bear right up road for 200 yards to junction on right (opposite The Plough). Turn right up lane to Abney for 300 yards and fork left on metalled farm track for 100 yards when you go left down through a copse and ahead to go left over a stream to enter a sloping field. Bear slightly left up by wall side to gate and ahead up track to a road. There are spectacular views here to the N of Win Hill and Bamford Edge. Turn right along farm road (W) soon to pass a farm and ahead through gate on a field path that is fairly well defined. After three fields we enter a wood, and shortly reach a hand-gate with a footbridge over Highlow Brook on the right.

Keep ahead up slope (SW) on a most pleasant path for ½ mile or so to drop down to Stoke Ford where the Bretton Brook joins the main stream. (An ideal spot for a picnic — but leave no litter please). We bear left here to go almost S with the Bretton Brook on our right on a winding grassy path that gradually leaves the sound of the brook. After nearly ½ mile we cross a stream and pass between remains of some farm buildings and continue SW on the terrace path for ⅓ mile to bend left to cross over another stream amidst trees. Keep left here up to reach a small flat area with a short length of wall to the right. Turn sharp left to climb steeply — zig-zagging up to reach a small open plateau from which there are fine views to the W.

Turn left along grassy path (S) a short distance — then right by stone wall by field-side (W) to field-gate with house on your left to reach a road. Keep ahead up road (SW) for ¼ mile to junction with *The Barrel Inn* to your left. From the 1200ft. contour level there are good views to the S. This PH has a reputation not only for refreshments but for being snowed up during the winter. I recollect the 1947 big freeze when the pub (a much more lowly establishment in those days) was isolated for several weeks.

Turn left along the road for 150 yards to FP on right to go down by wall side to stile, then steeply down across the contours making for the works ahead. When half-way through the fluorspar works, bear right down a road to join the classified road — then left for ¾ mile into Eyam village.

Eyam lies below Eyam Moor and is a village of tragedy created by the plague of 1665-6. The infection reached the village in some clothes sent from London to a local tailor who died within a few days. By the following year 257 villagers had died, the churchyard became full and burials took place on land outside. It was the rector, Wm. Mompesson, who persuaded most of the villagers to stay put to prevent spreading the disease further afield.

The village overlooks Middleton Dale whilst the surrounding hills are riddled with old lead mines and Burial mounds. As you reach the church you will see the 'Plague Cottages' on your left. In the churchyard there is a very well preserved Saxon cross, some 8ft. in height, which is said to be 1,000 years old. There is also much of interest in the church. The village is well served with shops and inns. The well-dressing ceremonies take place at the end of August and beginning of September. There is a YH to the N of the village street.

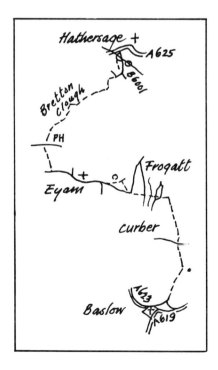

(Buses run between Chesterfield and Castleton, with a service to Bakewell on Mondays only).

Keep ahead (E) along the main street and , when almost at the end of the village, fork left along an asphalted lane sign-posted to 'Riley Graves'. The lane runs along a high terrace and after about ⅓rd mile you will see on your left a small walled enclosure of a burial ground of one of the families that were victims of the plague in 1666. Continue E along lane for 300 yards to bear right on FP down through a wood. Keep right at fork to go down a gulley and into a field where we dog-leg right/left to continue S with wall on left down to reach a road (B6521) on a bend.

Cross over to FP by field-gate and down field-side, go over stile and ahead to the Bakewell Road (B6001) at a 'T' junction. Cross over to go down lane (E) for ¼ mile to cross over the river Derwent via a 17th century bridge and into Froggatt village.

Froggatt is a small gritstone village lying immediately below a gritstone edge of the same name. There is a PH in the village.

Turn right for almost 200 yards — then left through stile by field-gate up a rough field to reach the main street. (The PH is a few yards to the left). Cross over road to a path that climbs steeply through trees to reach a track under the gritstone cliff. Turn right here to proceed in a southerley direction on a broad track which is never very far from the edge. There are most spectacular views to the S and W for the next 1¾ miles along Curbar and (later) Baslow Edge.

After a mile or so we cross over a road that comes up from Curbar village and continue S for ⅔ mile to the end of the ridge where the track bends right. At this point you will see the Wellington Monument some 100 yards to the left.

Follow the main track (SW) downhill and into the streets of Baslow. At the first junction keep ahead to reach the main road (A623) by the church in the centre of the village. (GR 252723)

Baslow is divided into three parts — Far End, Bridge End and Nether End. The church is mostly modern but the tower and steeple are 13th century. Some old coffin stones have been incorporated in the structure. A 17th century bridge crosses the Derwent a little to the W of the church. The village is well provided with shops, hotels and inns, and served by the Bakewell/Chesterfield bus service.

Day Ten

Baslow, Chatsworth Park, Edensor, Beeley, Calton Pastures, Bakewell

9 miles (Map – O.S. 1:50,000 119)

Start – GR 252723

FROM the church go E on the Chesterfield Road (A619) for ¼ mile to FP on right (opposite 'Alstonfields'), down steps, ahead over stone bridge to pass house on left and through kissing-gate into **Chatsworth Park** — an estate of the Duke of Devonshire. Keep ahead (S) for about a mile to pass an ornate stone pile — Queen Mary's Bower — prior to reaching road bridge on right. From the bridge we have a view of Chatsworth House to the E, and the course of the river Derwent midst an appreciable area of parkland to the S and W. This Palladian style house of the Cavendish family was partly built by Wm Talman from 1687 and completed by Thos. Archer in 1707. The house contains an outstanding private art collection and is open from Easter to the end of October, 11.30 a.m. to 4.30 p.m. The Deer Park was laid out by Capability Brown during the 18th century.

Immediately over the bridge, fork right on FP that cuts across the park, SW then W to Edensor village (pronounced — Ensor).

Edensor was re-built in the middle of the last century by the 6th Duke. The church dates from 1863 — the tower and spire were designed by Sir Gilbert Scott in the 14th century style. In the chancel there is brass to the memory of John Beton, a servant to Mary Queen of Scots who was 'housed' — if not imprisoned — in the Bower near the bridge. There is also an inscription to Sir Joseph Paxton who died in 1865. During his period of employment at Chatsworth he was responsible for the landscaping of the park and the construction of the huge conservatory — which was, alas, demolished in 1920. It was this structure that formed the basis for the design for the original Crystal Palace which was erected for the Great Exhibition of 1851 and was destroyed by fire in 1936. At various points in the Park you will see notice boards giving a brief history of the estate.

On leaving the estate village, turn right (SE) by roadside for 300 yards to a junction and keep ahead across parkland — gradually getting nearer the river which is duly reached after about ¾ mile when just short of a stone farm building. Ahead to Beeley Bridge — which is the southern boundary of the Park — where we turn left to go over the bridge. Some 200 yards ahead — when just beyond right bend — turn left by Beeley Lodge up a cul-de-sac lane to Beeley Hill

Top. At the top bear left for 100 yards by farm to FP on right that goes through farmyard. Make for the far right corner to enter field and keep by wall on left into the next field. At this point we have fine views to the S down the Derwent valley — with Beeley village below. Go half left down the next two fields, then follow hedgerow into Beeley.

Beeley is a most attractive small village with some fine 17th century houses. The church has a Norman doorway, 14th century tower with 15th century battlements and pinnacles. There is a shop, a post office and a pleasant hostelry — *The Devonshire Arms*.

We join the main road (B6012) near the PH to turn right along same N for 200 yards to a FP on left (opposite the church). The path goes diagonally across a large field for ½ mile to recross Beeley Bridge.

Just beyond house on left, fork up a narrow path into a car park (with toilets). Take road on left through field-gate S, soon to bend right into Calton Lees. After another right bend, keep ahead through field-gate on rough metalled road up the valley for ⅔ mile to zig-zag right/left to pass between farm buildings and a house at Calton Houses. Keep ahead to enter a field, where turn right up by fieldside for 350 yards until, when half-way across a large field, we leave the BW and turn left on the 'FP to Bakewell'. (A good viewpoint here of Beeley Moor to the E).

The footpath goes WNW on a broad grassy path for ⅓ mile to pass through field-gate into an even larger field. Keep ahead — almost parallel with plantations to right — aiming for a small copse on the skyline. Just of the trees is a pond where go left over stile an another just ahead. From this highest contour bear slightly left to pass a beech copse on your right and make for the lowest contour of the wall ahead which we cross by steps over same. Go steeply down through woodland to a cross track and stagger right, then left down to a broader track through trees and on to the golf course. Continue W

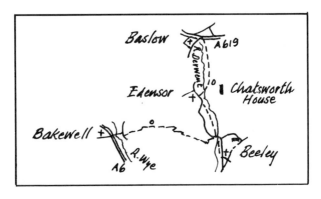

across the course to pass over the old railway line and ahead through gate and bear left down to a road. Turn right, then first left to the town bridge and into the centre of Bakewell. (GR 218686)

A few notes on Bakewell appear in the introduction.